SO-AHY-606

# City Leaves
# City Trees

The trees in this book are to be found in the New England, Middle Atlantic, and North Central states.

# City Leaves
# City Trees

## by EDWARD GALLOB

*Photographs and Photograms by the author*

CHARLES SCRIBNER'S SONS · NEW YORK

*For Tana and Miela*

The author wishes to express his appreciation to
Mrs. Florence Montgomery Givens, botanist,
Academy of Natural Sciences of Philadelphia,
for checking the manuscript for botanical accuracy
and for supplying the scientific names for the index.

This book published simultaneously in
the United States of America and in Canada —
Copyright under the Berne Convention

3 5 7 9 11 13 15 17 19  RD/C  20 18 16 14 12 10 8 6 4

Printed in the United States of America
Library of Congress Catalog Card Number 72-37187
SBN 684-12808-X (Trade,)

# CONTENTS

*How To Use This Book,* 6–9

*Trees with Simple-Alternate Leaves*

Leaves with Smooth Edges

MAGNOLIA, 10–11

Leaves with Toothed Edges

BASSWOOD, 12–13

ELM, 14–15

BIRCH, 16–17

BEECH, 18–19

CHERRY, 20–21

WILLOW, 22–23

POPLAR, 24–25

HAWTHORN, 26–27

HOLLY, 28–29

Leaves with Lobed Edges

TULIP TREE, 30–31

SYCAMORE, 32–33

Leaves with Lobed-Toothed Edges

SWEET GUM, 34–35

Oak Leaves with All Kinds of Edges

WHITE OAK, 36–37

CHESTNUT OAK, 37

PIN OAK, 38

SCARLET OAK, 38

WILLOW OAK, 39

RED OAK, 39

*Trees with Simple-Opposite Leaves*

Leaves with Smooth Edges

DOGWOOD, 40–41

CATALPA, 42–43

PRINCESS TREE, 42–43

*Trees with Simple-Opposite Leaves* Contd.

Leaves with Lobed Edges

RED MAPLE, 44–45

SILVER MAPLE, 44–45

SUGAR MAPLE, 46

NORWAY MAPLE, 47

*Trees with Compound-Alternate Leaves*

AILANTHUS, 48–49

HONEY LOCUST, 50–51

*Trees with Compound-Opposite Leaves*

ASH, 52–53

BOX ELDER, 52–53

HORSE CHESTNUT, 54–55

*Cone Trees with Needles, or Scalelike Leaves*

PINE, 56–57

LARCH, 56–57

FIR, 58

HEMLOCK, 58

SPRUCE, 58

ARBORVITAE, 59

EASTERN RED CEDAR, 59

*Tree with Leaves Different from All Others*

GINKGO, 60–61

*Collecting,* 62

*Making Leaf Photograms,* 62

*Index, including botanical names,* 63

# How To Use This Book

This book will help you identify the trees that grow around you in the city. For the most part, the trees of the forest are native American trees, but the trees of the city are—like its people—from many different parts of the world.

Start with the tree closest to you. Is it an elm, a spruce, or a ginkgo perhaps? To identify your tree, the first step is to match its leaves with one of the following groups.

Most trees can be divided into two large groups—depending on their kinds of leaves. One group has broad, flat leaves and the other group has needles, or scalelike leaves. This second group we call evergreens. Most trees with broad, flat leaves shed their leaves in autumn and are known as deciduous trees.

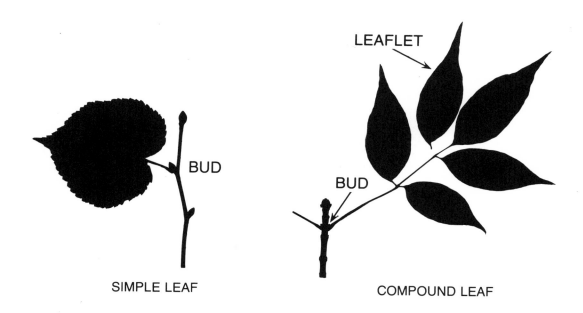

SIMPLE LEAF                          COMPOUND LEAF

A simple leaf has one single leaf blade. A compound leaf has many blades, called leaflets. Leaflets look like leaves, but note in the illustration above that the leaf has a bud where its stem joins the twig. A leaflet does not have a bud. A bud is the beginning of next year's growth, and is visible at all times except the late spring.

The edges of leaves and leaflets may be smooth, toothed, lobed, or lobed-toothed.

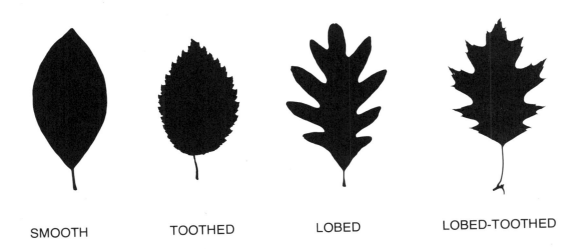

SMOOTH          TOOTHED          LOBED          LOBED-TOOTHED

The next thing to look for is how leaves grow in relation to each other along the twig of the tree. Most trees have *simple* leaves that grow in *alternate* places along the twig.

SIMPLE-ALTERNATE

If your leaf has a smooth edge, turn to page 10.
If your leaf has a toothed edge, see pages 12–29.
If your leaf has a lobed edge, see pages 30–33.
If your leaf has a lobed-toothed edge, turn to page 34.
Oak leaves are simple-alternate leaves with all kinds of edges. For oak leaves see pages 36–39.

The next group of trees has *simple* leaves that are *opposite* each other along the twig.

SIMPLE-OPPOSITE

If your leaf has a smooth edge, see pages 40–43.
If your leaf has a lobed edge, see pages 44–47.

A third group of trees has *compound* leaves that grow in *alternate* places along the twig. Look for these leaves on pages 48–51.

COMPOUND-ALTERNATE

And the last group of trees with broad, flat leaves has *compound* leaves that grow *opposite* to each other. See pages 52–55.

COMPOUND-OPPOSITE

A hand-shaped compound-opposite leaf is on pages 54–55.

Trees with needles or scalelike leaves are, for the most part, evergreen trees. They have cones and most of them belong to the Pine family. Christmas trees are in this group. To identify trees of this kind, turn to pages 56–59.

NEEDLES OR SCALELIKE

If your leaf does not match any in this book, you have a mystery tree. Perhaps you can solve the mystery at the library, where they have books on all the trees.

In the beginning naming trees may appear to be difficult. There are so many trees and many of them seem to look alike. But in time you will become aware of the differences. Besides the leaf pattern, trees differ in the feel of the bark, the shape and size of the tree, the pattern of the branches, the look of the bud, flower, and fruit, and sometimes in the fragrance of the crushed leaf.

*Oriental Magnolia*

# MAGNOLIA

Magnolias have large, simple-alternate leaves with smooth edges. The winter buds are plump and hairy. The fruits resemble small green cucumbers. When ripe, they release red seeds that hang by thin threads. Oriental Magnolias blossom in the spring before they are in leaf. The large, cup-shaped flowers are white, pink, or purple. American Magnolias blossom in the summer after the leaves are out. The Southern Magnolia, an evergreen tree, has large, thick leaves, glossy-green on top and fuzzy-brown below. Its wide, white blossoms are the largest of the tree flowers. Common in the South, it is rare and treasured in the North, growing only in sheltered places.

10

WINTER BUD

FRUIT

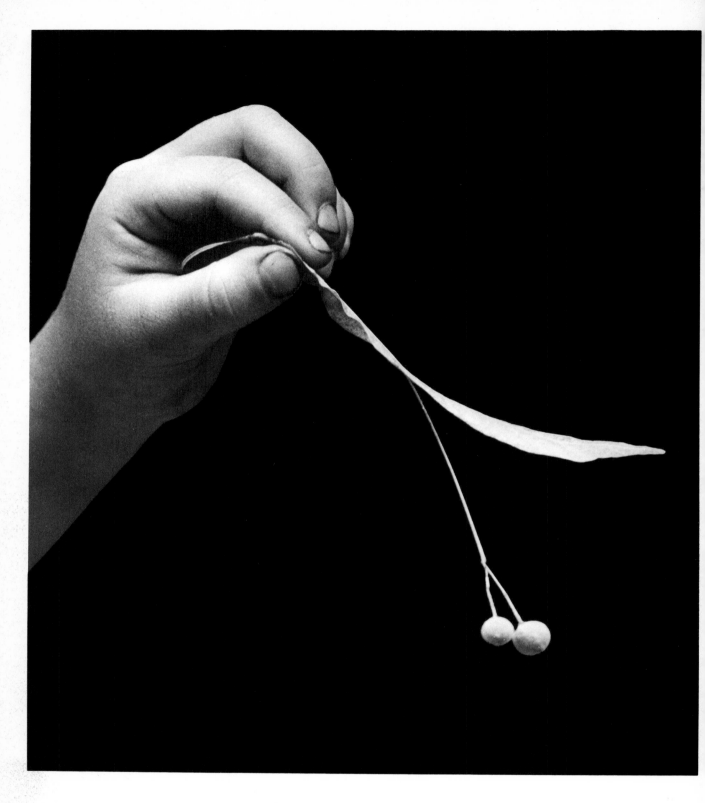

# BASSWOOD

The Basswood, or American Linden, is a spreading shade tree. Its large leaves are simple-alternate with fine-toothed edges. They are heart-shaped with a lopsided base. The bark on young trees is dark-brown and smooth; on older trees it is dark-gray and furrowed. Fragrant, creamy-white flowers develop into small nutlets. They hang in clusters, attached by a slender stem to the underside of a narrow, leafy wing. There are many Lindens, but the American Linden has the largest leaf. Bees make honey from the abundant nectar of the Linden blossom, giving it the name "bee tree."

12

FLOWERS

FRUIT

*American Elm*

# ELM

The Elm has simple-alternate, lopsided, egg-shaped leaves, with rough-toothed edges. It is one of the first trees to flower in the spring. The fruits are paper-thin ovals with the seed in the center. The American Elm grows to be a very large tree. The dark, furrowed trunk divides one third of the way up into a few stout branches, looking somewhat like the letter *Y*. Once our most common shade tree, it is now threatened with extinction by the Dutch elm disease. The Slippery Elm has leaves similar to those of the American Elm, but its seeds are larger. Its name comes from the slippery surface of its inner bark.

AMERICAN ELM FRUIT

SLIPPERY ELM
FRUIT

# BIRCH

The bark of all Birches has strong cross markings. The simple-alternate shiny leaves are egg-shaped or triangle-shaped with uneven teeth. Pollen-bearing catkins hang from branches in the spring. The fruit, which looks like a small cone, is a stack of flat oval seeds that falls apart in the winter. The names of the different Birch trees describe their bark: Gray, White, Black, or Yellow. Real birch beer is brewed from the twigs of the Black Birch tree. Indians peeled the waterproof bark from the American White (or Paper) Birch to cover their canoes. Once a Birch tree has been stripped of its bark, the bark does not grow back.

PAPER BIRCH

POLLEN
CATKIN

GRAY BIRCH

FRUIT
CONE

EUROPEAN WHITE BIRCH

# BEECH

Beech trees are good for climbing. The spreading branches grow close to the ground. The leaf, bark, bud, and fruit identify the Beech. The simple alternate leaves are silky smooth with coarse teeth, one tooth for each vein. The bark of the Beech tree is a smooth light-gray. The brown winter buds are long and pointed. The fruit is a small triangular nut in a husky pod and is good to eat. Real beechnut flavor comes from these nuts. If you find a Beech tree in your neighborhood or park, keep an eye on the nuts as they ripen. Get to them before the birds do.

18

WINTER BUDS

FRUIT

*Oriental Flowering Cher..*

# CHERRY

Cherry trees have narrow, single-alternate leaves with even-toothe
edges. The bark has raised, horizontal markings. The Japanese Flowerir
Cherry is one of the Oriental Cherry trees that is planted for its blossoms ar
does not bear fruit. Two of the American fruit-bearing Cherry trees are th
Pin and the Chokecherry, with small white flowers and fruits that grow
clusters. These trees are found in left-alone places, of which there a
still some in every city. Look for wild cherries in July.

FLOWERS

CHOKECHERRY

FLOWERING CHERRY

*Black Willow*

# WILLOW

Willows have simple-alternate, short-stemmed, narrow leaves. The flower and fruit of the Willow is a catkin. Willows are easy to tell from other trees, but it is difficult to tell one kind of Willow from another. The Weeping Willow, from Asia, is planted more than any other Willow. It has long pointed leaves and drooping yellow branches that move with the wind. The Black Willow is the largest American Willow. Willows prefer to grow where the soil is moist, especially along streams. If you cut a Willow branch and place it in water, it will develop roots in a few weeks and will be ready to plant.

BLACK WILLOW

*Lombardy Poplar*

# POPLAR

The Lombardy Poplar, with triangle-shaped leaves, grows rapidly—tall and straight. Soft, hugging branches cover the tree trunk from the ground up. Poplars are related to the Willows. The family flower is a hanging catkin that looks like a caterpillar. The Carolina Poplar, or Cottonwood tree, is large and stout and is apt to be found in the older parts of town where it was planted for its rapid growth. It is no longer planted in many cities because of its short life and its tendency to litter the street with flower seeds and brittle branches.

LOMBARDY
POPLAR

CAROLINA
POPLAR

POLLEN
CATKIN

*Washington Hawthorn*

# HAWTHORN

Hawthorns have thorns. They are the only simple-leafed trees that have thorns on their twigs and branches. Locust trees have thorns, but the leaves of the locust are compound. Hawthorn trees are small and bushy. There are many different kinds of Hawthorns, with a great variety of leaves. Even the leaves on the same tree may vary.

White or pink clustered flowers bloom in the late spring. The red or yellow fruits, resembling small apples, remain on the tree all winter, providing food for birds.

26

FRUIT

FLOWER

# HOLLY

Holly is traditionally associated with Christmas. The name *Holly* is probably a corruption of the word *holy*. It used to be called the Holy tree because of its usage at the time of Christmas in the churches. It is a small evergreen tree with simple-alternate leaves and red berries. The thick leaf has a wavy edge with spiny teeth. In the spring the tree bears small white flowers.

FRUIT

# TULIP TREE

The Tulip tree, or Yellow Poplar, has simple-alternate, square-shaped leaves with a unique, broad notch at the top. Its large, greenish-yellow flowers are like tulips. They bloom in May and June. The dry fruit is a cone of overlapping, narrow wings. These winged seeds are released one by one throughout the winter months. The red winter bud is a small oval pouch that holds the growing leaf. When ready, the leaf comes out in a folded position.

In the forest the Tulip tree grows to a great size, sometimes as high as one hundred feet.

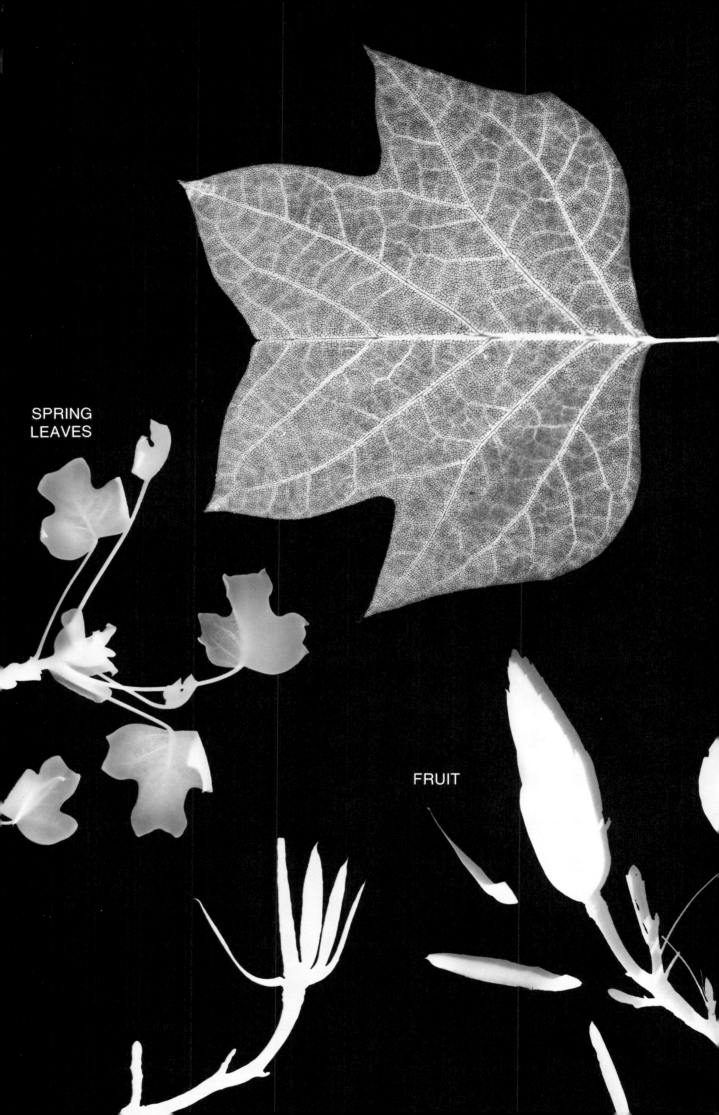

SPRING
LEAVES

FRUIT

# SYCAMORE

The Sycamore is also known as the Buttonwood or the Plane tree. The Sycamore, one of our largest trees, is planted in great numbers as a shade tree. The leaves, shaped like the maple leaf, are alternate on the twig instead of opposite as on the maple tree. The leaves are thick, with fuzzy undersides. The Sycamore can also be identified by its mottled bark and button-ball fruit. Its outer, dark-brown bark peels in patches, exposing its light underbark. The button-ball fruits hang by long stems from the tree throughout the winter. In the spring the fruits break, covering the ground with countless tiny, hairy, brown seeds.

FRUIT

SEEDS

# SWEET GUM

The Sweet Gum is a tall tree, originating in the South, with simple alternate lobed leaves. The sap of the tree produces a yellow gum with sweet smell. Crush some of the star-shaped leaves in your hand and sme the spicy fragrance.

The fruit of the Sweet Gum is a long-stemmed round ball, covere with sharp points. Each point is a capsule of tiny seeds. From a distance th hanging fruit resembles the Sycamore's. The bark grows in corky ridges o twigs and branches. Because of this the Sweet Gum is sometimes called th "alligator tree."

34

TWIG

FRUIT

SPRING LEAVES
AND FLOWER

# OAK

There are more Oaks than any other kind of tree. All mature Oaks have acorns. If you find acorns under a tree, it is probably an Oak tree. Oaks are grouped according to the shapes of their leaves and the time in which their acorns mature. The White Oak group has lobed leaves without points and the bark is usually light and smooth. Their sweet acorns mature in one year and the shells are hairless inside.

The leaves of the Black (sometimes referred to as Red) Oak group have pointed lobes with bristle tips. Their acorns are bitter and mature in two years, and the shells are hairy inside.

CHESTNUT
OAK

POLLEN
FLOWERS

ACORN

WHITE
OAK

SCARLET OAK

ACORN

ACORN

PIN OAK

# PIN OAK AND SCARLET OAK

The leaves of the Pin Oak and the Scarlet Oak are alike. The difference in size and shape of their mature acorns will help in identification. The lower branches of the Pin Oak grow downward. The leaves of the Scarlet Oak turn scarlet in autumn.

RED OAK

ACORN

ACORN

WILLOW OAK

# WILLOW OAK AND RED OAK

The Willow Oak has the leaf of the Willow and the acorn of the Oak.
Each leaf has one bristle tooth at its tip. The acorn is round as a ball.

The Red Oak's leaf is wide and full and turns red in the autumn. Its
acorn is large and plump with a shallow cup.

*Flowering Dogwood*

# DOGWOOD

The small Flowering Dogwood is one of the few trees with simple-opposite leaves. The veins of the leaf follow its oval shape. Winter buds, like tiny mushrooms, sit on the end of the twigs. White flowers with four petals bloom early in the spring. In midsummer the flower is replaced by a tight cluster of green berries that turn red in the fall.

In the forest the Dogwood grows in the shade of larger trees. If you stand under a Dogwood tree and look up at its branches, you will see that they spread out in a matching mirror pattern.

WINTER BUD

FLOWERS

FRUIT

*Princess Tree*

# CATALPA AND PRINCESS TREE

The leaves of the Catalpa and the Princess tree are alike. They are the only large trees with simple-opposite heart-shaped leaves. They both have large, clustered cones of flowers. The Catalpa flower is white and that of the Princess tree is purple.

Catalpa fruits are long, thin, dark pods packed with long, fuzzy seeds. Princess tree pods are pecan-shaped and filled with very small seeds. The pods of both trees remain on the tree throughout the winter and early spring.

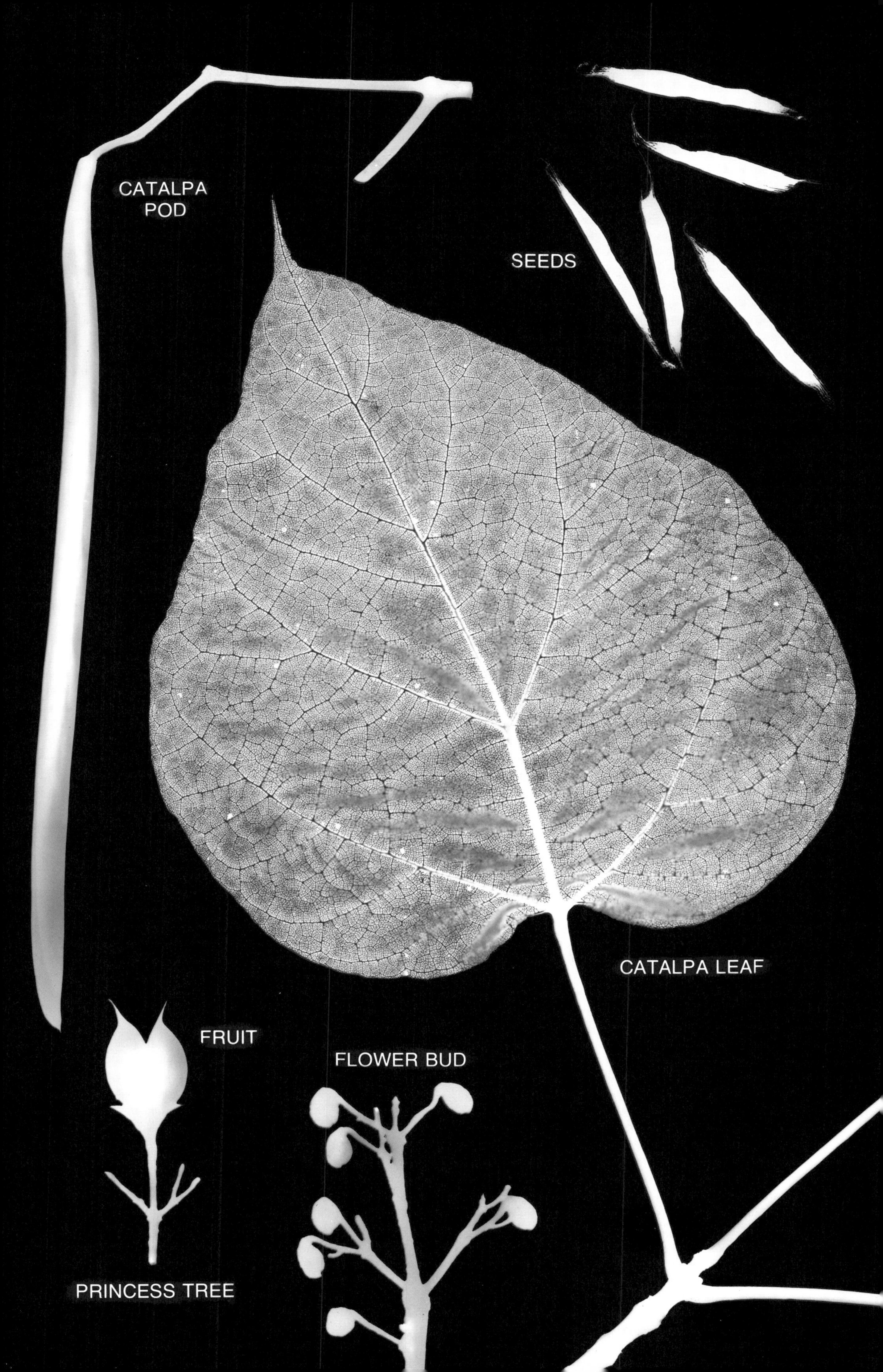

CATALPA
POD

SEEDS

FRUIT

FLOWER BUD

CATALPA LEAF

PRINCESS TREE

# MAPLE

Maples are easy to identify. They are the only large trees with simple opposite leaves that are lobed. The fruits, called keys, are a pair of curved wings that separate in two parts. Each part has one seed. Red Maple leaves are three-lobed. The middle lobe is longest. The spring flowers, first leaves, seed keys, and autumn leaves of the Red Maple are all red. Silver Maple leaves are bright-green on top, silvery below. The lobes are deeply cut. The bark of old Silver Maple trees is dark-gray and is separated in large, shaggy flakes.

RED MAPLE

FRUIT

SILVER MAPLE

FRUIT

FRUIT

# SUGAR MAPLE

The small Sugar Maple key is plump, and its wings grow close together. The larger Norway Maple key is outstretched. Maple syrup is made from the boiled-down sap of the Sugar Maple. In the spring, under these trees you may find sprouted keys. If you do, try planting one in a small flowerpot.

FLOWER

FRUIT

# NORWAY MAPLE

The Norway Maple is the most common Maple in the city. In the spring it has large clusters of yellow-green flowers that look like leaves. The leaves of the Norway Maple and the Sugar Maple are similar. However, the Norway Maple leaf is wide, and the Sugar Maple leaf is long. The stem of the Norway Maple exudes a milky sap when broken. The sap of the Sugar Maple is clear.

# AILANTHUS

The Ailanthus, which was brought to this country from Europe, is a native tree of China. It is sometimes called the "tree of Heaven." No one seems to plant an Ailanthus. They grow very quickly in city yards, empty lots, near fences and buildings—wherever the trees' many seeds can find soil. The Ailanthus has a very long, compound-alternate leaf. The large leaflets have smooth edges with two small teeth at the base. The tree's twisted, narrow-winged fruits each have one seed in the middle. Large reddish clusters of fruits, formed late in the summer, turn brown later on and hang on the tree throughout the winter and spring.

FLOWERS

FRUIT

# HONEY LOCUST

The Honey Locust has long compound-alternate leaves. Sometimes the leaflets themselves are compound. It is difficult to climb a Honey Locust because of the many large thorns on the trunk and branches. These thorns can be used as fish hooks and pins. The fruit is a long, twisted bean pod which turns dark when it is ripe. Inside is a sweet green pulp. Taste it.

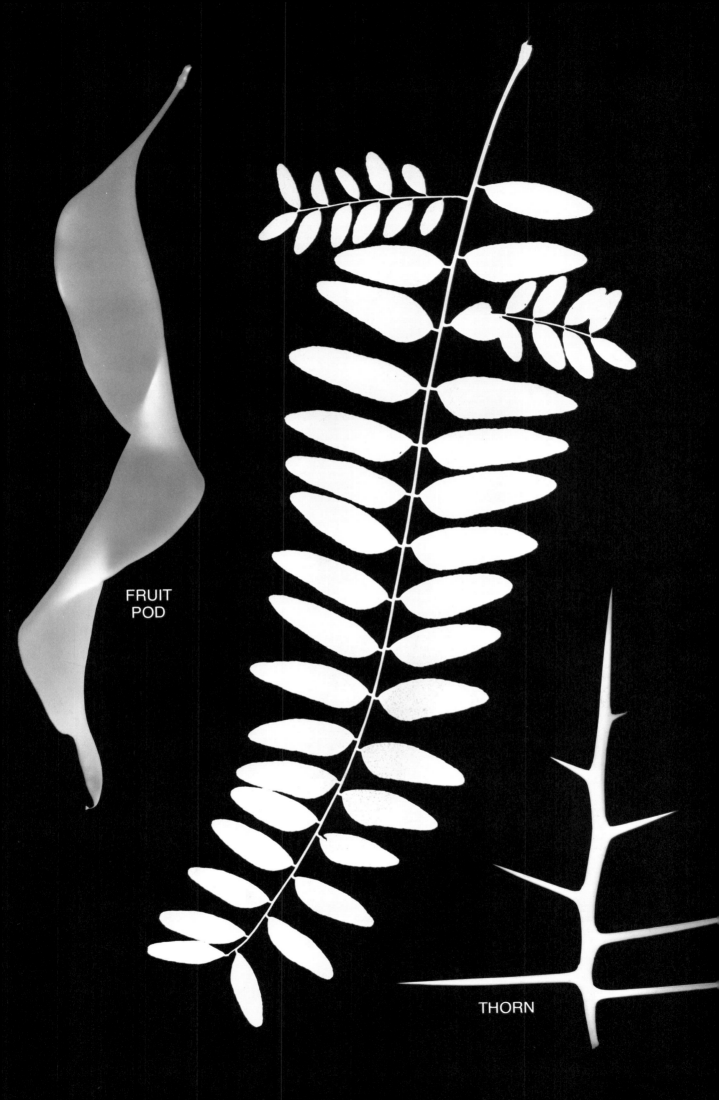

FRUIT
POD

THORN

*Ash tree*

# ASH AND BOX ELDER

The Ash and the Box Elder are the only native American trees with compound-opposite leaves. The Ash has long, droopy leaves with short-stemmed leaflets. Its purple flowers grow in tight clusters close to the twig. The fruits, found only on the female tree, have narrow flat wings with the seed at one end.

Though the leaf of the Box Elder is like that of the Ash, its fruit is like a double-winged Maple key. Since trees are grouped in families according to their fruit, the Box Elder is also known as the Ashleaf Maple and belongs to the Maple family.

52

BOX ELDER

FRUIT

FRUIT

ASH

# HORSE CHESTNUT

The leaves of the Horse Chestnut are compound-opposite. It is the only tree whose leaflets grow like the outstretched fingers of your hand—all connected at one point. The spring buds are plump and sticky. Large clusters of white flowers bloom in May and June. The nut of the Horse Chestnut, contained in a prickly husk, is bitter and should not be eaten. The roasted chestnuts sold on city streets are another variety, related to beechnuts. Some people believe a polished chestnut (of any variety) brings good luck.

Horse Chestnut trees were brought here from Europe. Their native American relative is the Buckeye.

FLOWER

FRUIT

SEED

*Red Pine*

# PINE AND LARCH

Most evergreen trees with cones belong to the Pine family. Besides the true Pine, other members of the Pine family are the Larch, Spruce, Fir, Hemlock, and Cedar. Pine leaves are needlelike and grouped in clusters of two to five. Each cluster is wrapped in a sheath at the twig. The Pine fruit is a dry cone, made up of overlapping scales. When the mature cone opens, loose seeds fall out.

The Larch, or Tamarack, is the only member of the Pine family that is not an evergreen tree. In autumn it drops its spiral of needles and is bare all winter.

WHITE PINE

LEAF CLUSTER

CONE

LARCH

AUSTRIAN PINE

SEED

CONE

SPRUCE

HEMLOCK

CONE

FIR

# FIR, HEMLOCK, AND SPRUCE

Fir and Hemlock needles have two white lines on their undersides. Fir needles curl upward. The upright cones of Fir trees drop their scales all at once. Hemlock needles are in flat, feathery rows. Small cones hang at the tips of the Hemlock branches.

The Spruce needles have four sides and stick out from all sides of the twig. The hanging cones of the Spruce fall off in one piece.

FRUIT

EASTERN RED CEDAR

ARBORVITAE

# ARBORVITAE AND
# EASTERN RED CEDAR

The Arborvitae, or Northern White Cedar, has flattened stems covered with scalelike leaves.

The Eastern Red Cedar is a Juniper. Its fruit is a bluish berry. The leaves are either scalelike or short and pointed.

# GINKGO

Ginkgo trees are special. They have been around longer than any other tree and were here in prehistoric times. Ginkgoes were brought to this country from Asia. The leaves are fan-shaped and grow in small clusters from a short, blunt spur. Ginkgoes are planted in great numbers in city streets because they've been found to be smog and disease resistant.

Although the fruit of the Ginkgo smells bad, it contains a large, plum-like nut that is good to eat when roasted. In the autumn the leaves of the Ginkgo turn yellow.

FRUIT

SEED

KERNEL

# Collecting

Each tree has a time of year when it is best to collect its things. Tree things are leaves, twigs, flowers, fruit, and seeds. For the Elm seed, early in the spring. For the Oak, acorns in the autumn. By then the leaves are full-grown and the insects have not started to eat them. No two leaves of any tree are exactly alike—they will differ in size and shape.

Select leaves from mature branches, avoiding young shoots near the ground. A plastic bag with a few drops of water inside is good for gathering. Press the leaves as soon as possible in a book or between newspaper sheets or blotters. Change the paper or turn the leaves every day until they're dry. Mount the leaves and other tree things on construction paper or any stiff paper with white glue. Indicate on each sheet the name of the tree, its location, date of collection, and your name. You may like to make a photograph or a drawing of your tree to go with each sheet.

Arrange a visit to your nature museum to see their leaf collection. Be the first in your neighborhood to identify all its trees.

# Making Leaf Photograms

The leaf illustrations in this book are actually photograms, or shadow photographs. Photograms are made in a darkroom and are the simplest kind of photographic image to create. To make photograms of leaves, place the leaves directly on photographic paper and expose it to light. The light should come from one source, such as a photo enlarger or a clear bulb. A forty-watt bulb at a distance of three feet from a sheet of enlarging paper with a light exposure of one second is a good way to start. To reproduce more detail in the leaf keep the light on longer.

Photograms can also be made on blueprint paper without a darkroom using the same procedure but substituting the sun as the light source. In subdued light place the leaves directly on the blue side of the paper. Hold in place with a sheet of glass and expose to bright sunlight. When the exposed blue paper turns white, quickly submerge the print in a pan of water or a solution of one part 3% hydrogen peroxide and eight parts water until the print is completely reversed. Pat with paper towels and lay out to dry.

# INDEX

Ailanthus (*Ailanthus altissima*), 48, 49

Arborvitae (*Thuja occidentalis*), 59

Ash (*Fraxinus*), 52, 53

Basswood (*Tilia americana*), 12, 13

Beech (*Fagus grandifolia*), 18, 19

Birch

    American White Birch. *See* Paper Birch

    Black Birch (*Betula lenta*), 16

    European White Birch (*Betula pendula*), 17

    Gray Birch (*Betula populifolia*), 16, 17

    Paper Birch (*Betula papyrifera*), 16, 17

    Yellow Birch (*Betula lutea*), 16

Box Elder (*Acer negundo*), 52, 53

Buckeye. *See* Horse Chestnut

Buttonwood. *See* Sycamore

Catalpa (*Catalpa bignonioides*), 42, 43

Cedar

    Eastern Red Cedar (*Juniperus virginiana*), 59

    Northern White Cedar. *See* Arborvitae

Cherry

    Chokecherry (*Prunus virginiana*), 20, 21

    Oriental Flowering Cherry, 20, 21

    Pin Cherry (*Prunus pennsylvanica*), 20

Cottonwood. *See* Poplar, Carolina

Dogwood, Flowering (*Cornus florida*), 40, 41

Elm

    American Elm (*Ulmus americana*), 14, 15

    Slippery Elm (*Ulmus rubra*), 14, 15

Fir (*Abies*), 56, 58

Ginkgo (*Ginkgo biloba*), 60, 61

Hawthorn (*Crataegus*), 26, 27

Hemlock (*Tsuga canadensis*), 56, 58

Holly (*Ilex*), 28, 29

Horse Chestnut (*Aesculus hippocastanum*), 54, 55

Juniper. *See* Cedar, Eastern Red

Larch (*Larix*), 56, 57

Linden. *See* Basswood

Locust, Honey (*Gleditsia triacanthos*), 50, 51

Magnolia

    Oriental Magnolia, 10, 11

    Southern Magnolia (*Magnolia grandiflora*), 10

Maple

    Ashleaf Maple. *See* Box Elder

    Norway Maple (*Acer platanoides*), 46, 47

    Red Maple (*Acer rubrum*), 44, 45

    Silver Maple (*Acer saccharinum*), 44, 45

    Sugar Maple (*Acer saccharum*), 46, 47

Oak

    Chestnut Oak (*Quercus prinus*), 37

    Pin Oak (*Quercus palustris*), 38

    Red Oak (*Quercus rubra*), 36, 39

    Scarlet Oak (*Quercus coccinea*), 38

    White Oak (*Quercus alba*), 36, 37

    Willow Oak (*Quercus phellos*), 39

Pine

    Austrian Pine (*Pinus nigra*), 57

    Red Pine (*Pinus resinosa*), 56

    White Pine (*Pinus strobus*), 57

Plane tree. *See* Sycamore

Poplar

    Carolina Poplar (*Populus deltoides*), 24, 25

    Lombardy Poplar (*Populus nigra*), 24, 25

    Yellow Poplar. *See* Tulip tree

Princess tree (*Paulownia tomentosa*), 42, 43


Spruce (*Picea*), 56, 58

Sweet Gum (*Liquidambar styraciflua*), 34

Sycamore (*Platanus*), 32, 33


Tamarack. *See* Larch

"Tree of Heaven." *See* Ailanthus

Tulip tree (*Liriodendron tulipifera*), 30, 31


Willow

    Black Willow (*Salix nigra*), 22, 23

    Weeping Willow (*Salix babylonica*), 22